I0468822

How To Implement A Profit Sharing Plan

JOHN MILLAR

ISBN: 153063539X
ISBN-13: 9781530635399

DEDICATION

I dedicate this book to my mother and father, who raised me while self-employed. They taught me to work hard and listen to everyone but to make my own choices as to what is right and what is wrong.. and oh, did I mention work hard?

Anyone who tells you to work smart not hard hasn't ever done it tough and realized that if you work smart AND hard you will achieve more than you can possibly dream.

CONTENTS

1 HOW TO CREATE A PROFIT SHARING PLAN THAT MOTIVATES YOUR EMPLOYEES AND DRIVES REVENUE

A smart CEO understands that employee performance is tied directly to how vested they feel to the company they work for. That's why many companies have begun to consider profit sharing plans, because they can be a powerful incentive for employees to work harder for the company and gain a sense of satisfaction from knowing they'll all get a cut of the profits. It's also likely that the added productivity will increase the overall financial performance of the company.

Sue Holloway, an expert in compensation at WorldatWork, a human resources organization focused on employee benefits, explains that the objective of a profit sharing plan "is to foster employee identification with the organization's success." By implementing such a program, the CEO is saying, "We're all in this together, and everybody's focused on profit," says Holloway.

Recent statistics show just how popular variable pay programs, including profit sharing plans, have become. Eighty percent of businesses surveyed by WorldatWork reported having some sort of incentive or bonus program in 2009. So how do you make sure your plan will achieve financial results for your company, while increasing employee productivity and morale?

First, make sure you're profitable. And make sure you expect to continue making money for at least the next three years, to the best of what you can anticipate, says David Wray, president of the Profit Sharing/401k Council of America, a national nonprofit association of 1,200 companies committed to those employee benefits. "If you announce the plan and you have no profit sharing for a couple of years, it loses its credibility as a motivating force," Wray explains. "If you have a bad year and you don't pay that year, then people usually get it."

If you are profitable, here's what you need to consider when choosing and implementing a successful profit sharing plan.

Notes:

2 IMPLEMENTING A PROFIT SHARING PLAN: DETERMINE YOUR PURPOSE

The most important step in implementing a successful profit sharing plan is to have a clear idea of what you want to accomplish through the initiative. Various plans serve very particular purposes. Traditional profit sharing plans are designed as a retirement benefit. Employers contribute a specific, predetermined amount of their annual profits into a deferred trust, which the employees earn access to upon retirement from the company. This type of profit sharing plan suits companies with an aging workforce. You can achieve higher participation in a deferred profit sharing plan, if most of your workers are considering how they will fund their retirements. If you're looking to attract top-level senior executives, a deferred profit sharing plan can lure talented executive recruits, and also keep them working for you longer, as they will not be able to achieve full ownership of their trust until a specific date. And if you have a 401(k) program already in place, many employers combine that trust with their profit sharing plan and save on administrative costs.

If you're simply looking for a way to motivate your employees, a traditional, deferred profit sharing plan may not be the easiest way, says human resources specialist and a compensation expert Roberta Matuson, founder and president of Human Resource Solutions located in Northampton, Massachusetts. It requires a fair amount of paper work and is subject to regulation by the IRS. You are allowed to decide on a yearly basis what amount you want to contribute, or if you want to contribute at all, but the maximum annual contribution is $49,000, or 25 percent of an employee's compensation. There are also rules concerning who's eligible: 70 percent of your work force between the ages of 21 and 65, with one year of service, must participate, although there are some exceptions. An annual filing of the 5500 Form is also usually required, vesting is regulated, and the plan must not favor higher-compensated employees.

Your other choice is a cash profit sharing plan, which is not a retirement plan, and has become increasingly common. In this plan, an employee's predetermined share of the profits is paid directly in cash or check (sometimes stock), and those bonuses are taxed as a part of an employee's overall wages (unlike a deferred plan). Employers have a lot more leeway to establish the rules for their program and to determine who's eligible and how much they are paid out of the profits. The cash plan also typically appeals to a younger-skewing workforce, or one that tends to live paycheck to paycheck.

Notes:

3 IMPLEMENTING A PROFIT SHARING PLAN: DRAFTING A COMPREHENSIVE PLAN

Any successful plan will have clearly defined written terms, but there's plenty to consider when drafting the document. "What I've found with profit sharing programs, is that if they're not really thought through, they can become a huge negative," Matuson says. One way to avoid this is to make sure you solicit input not only from the experts, but also from within. Include all sectors of your company in the discussion, as they'll all be getting a share of the profits. The process of drafting your profit sharing plan is highly individual and should cater to your company's individual needs and goals. Some of the most successful profit sharing and bonus programs have evolved each year as the CEOs of those companies fine tune different aspects of the plans that aren't working each year.

You need to decide upon the formula in which you will allocate the profits among employees. For example, it's typical for companies to determine that 10 to 15 percent of their pre-tax profits will be eligible for distribution. "Every company has to look at their own way of operating and recognize their own realities," Wray says. "You have to look hard at your balance sheet and income." You also might want to consider setting a specific revenue target to meet in order to contribute to the profit sharing pool. Think about your shareholders too, and make sure that you still have enough earnings to allow for the company to increase in value.

Another issue to decide beforehand is the eligibility of your employees. Some profit sharing plans are only targeted toward the management level, although a deferred plan requires the eligibility of all employees. How much each employee earns, as a percentage of their compensation, can also be different with the cash plan. Although, make sure the percentages are equal if you choose a deferred plan, as you will be subject to annual nondiscrimination testing by the IRS

Jack Stack, CEO of Springfield, Missouri, based remanufacturer SRC Holdings and co-author with Bo Burlingham of A Stake in the Outcome: Building a Culture of Ownership for the Long-Term Success of Your Business, has a bonus plan similar to a cash profit sharing plan. He allocates a slightly different maximum for hourly and salaried employees. And while distribution of profits usually occurs annually, it doesn't always have to: he distributes quarterly, which serves as a more immediate reminder of the benefits of the program for employees.

You also want to consider how employees who leave the company before the allocation date will be paid, if at all. Many plans have provisions that require employment at the time of allocation to receive profits, so that you aren't giving a share of your profits to someone who quit nine months prior.

Ari Weinzweig, CEO of the Zingerman's Community of Businesses, an Ann Arbor, Michigan-based group of local food specialty businesses, learned to specify that, in order for employees to be paid under the group's plan, the business would need to have cash available, because profitable years can occur with restricted cash flow.

Choose your vesting schedule: whether you want employees to acquire gradual ownership, or whether you want to set a certain date in which they receive 100 percent of their trust. And finally, if you select a deferred profit sharing plan, make sure you fill out the proper documentation for the IRS and follow their guidelines

Notes:

4 IMPLEMENTING A PROFIT SHARING PLAN: EDUCATE AND COMMUNICATE

Insert chapter four text here. Insert chapter four text here. One of the biggest problems with a profit sharing plan is that people don't know how they can individually influence the overall profit of their company, Stack says. "If you have a highly profitable year, everyone gets to participate in the profit sharing program, but nobody learns anything about the company or what they did to influence that profit." To make your plan successful, educating your employees is crucial.

This can even be as basic as making

sure they understand the principles behind profits, and how they work, Wray says. Even though front-line employees in administration or accounting may not control many factors that lead to profitability, such as marketing and pricing of products and services, part of the implementation of the profit sharing plan should seek to educate them of their community role, beyond their narrow job description, he says.

Paul Spiegelman, CEO of the Bedford, Texas-based Beryl Companies, which provide call center services to the health care industry, found that his call advisers liked their bonus program, but didn't know how they specifically contributed to profitability. So, he included client retention, the percentage of client revenue his company retains from prior years, as a specific goal of the program to remind those employees that their performance is closely tied to overall profitability.

The education is part of an ongoing communication process that is necessary to maintain a successful profit sharing plan. Without frequently communicating to your employees about what the company is trying to accomplish, and what the revenue targets are and how close they are to being met, the plan can become routine and a share of the profits can even become expected. "The worst thing that happens is, in a down year, when there are no profits, people are angry and upset because they don't know what happened," Stack says. By communicating to them how the process works, you can combat any potential sense of entitlement amongst your employees. Open-book management, in which employees have extensive knowledge of the company's financial information, can be an effective strategy for helping employees understand the process.

Dig Deeper: Open-Book

Notes:

5 IMPLEMENTING A PROFIT SHARING PLAN: CONSIDER ALTERNATIVES

A cash or deferred profit sharing plan isn't your only option for sharing your profits with your employees. Those plans tend to focus on the broadly based metric of overall profitability of the company, and the collaborative success of the company. There are more loosely defined bonus programs that are closely tied to the same idea of sharing a company's profitability with its employees. Unlike other bonus programs, such as holiday bonuses, they set predetermined operational targets much in the same way as profit sharing programs do. Only these alternative bonus programs target specific financial ratios, like cash flow or diversification, and factor in the individual performance of an employee or a specific division.

Stack recognized that by putting in an incentive program that only targeted profitability, there was less focus on other weaknesses of his company. For example, when the credit markets froze up last year, he realized that there wasn't enough emphasis on cash flow, and that the growth of his company was tied to the accessibility of credit. So, that year's program set out to increase the cash flow numbers and educated employees in how they could contribute. "We wanted to put in an incentive program that would be an insurance policy; we were working on the weaknesses of the company and driving an incentive to fix those weaknesses, and use it as an education program to teach people how they make a difference in the company," Stack says. "Every year, we have a different incentive program, so it continually creates excitement and also builds upon the value of the company."

Likewise, Weinzweig used to have profit sharing plans for each one of his seven food specialty businesses comprising

Zingerman's Community of Businesses, but has since switched to gain sharing plans, that are specifically tailored to each company.

Notes:

ABOUT THE AUTHOR

John Millar has successfully owned and run multiple businesses since 1987, currently owns 3 businesses, it is this hands on experience that allows John to better understand and coach his clients.

In 2010 an internationally recognized Business Coaching group ranked John in the top 50 of over 1300 business coaches globally proving he is a leader in his industry.

In the last few years John has spoken to innumerable of business owners in Thailand, Hong Kong, Macau, China, South Korea, Japan, Hawaii and the USA, oh and his home country of Australia.

John has multiple formal business qualifications in Management, Human Resource Management, is a qualified NLP Practitioner, a Certified Trainer and Assessor AND is one of only 25 people in the world who is recognized as an Elite Business Trainer.

John has written a number of best-selling books and videos that are available on Amazon he has over a dozen audio books available on Audible.

John was a finalist in the:

Australian Institute of Management

Business Excellence Awards for an Owner Manager and this year has been nominated as 2015

Business Manager of the year.

John is also currently a:
Nominee in the 2015 Telstra Business Awards
Nominee in the 2015 Small Business Awards
Nominee in the 2015 IPPY Award
Finalist in the 2015 Axiom Business Book Award
Nominee in the 2015 Australian Small Business Champion Award

With experience, credentials and recognition like that it's no wonder he is a highly sought after Business Coach.

If you are ready to be coached by one of the best in the business, register at:
www.ceo-ondemand.com.au
Make sure to visit www.moreprofitlesstime.com and www.moreprofitlesstime.net for the new online Management Development Program: The Business Essentials Series.

ACCLAIM FOR JOHN MILLAR'S
Business Coaching and Training in their own words....

"Without John Millar as my Business Coach I wouldn't have a business today."
—Grant Jennings Managing Director, Jigsaw Projects
"Taking the decision to be coached and trained by John Millar was carefully considered after experiencing those who over promised and under delivered. I am pleased to say the content of his courses are the tools we all need to master as business owners. His delivery is engaging, thought provoking and empowering and after every session I came away re-energised. John always makes himself available for business building advice both

via Skype and face to face beyond the scope of delivery. With his extensive personal experience in building small businesses, he knows and understands what it takes to establish and grow a business.I have no hesitation endorsing John Millar as an educator and business coach and the bonus is he is a very nice person."

—Anne Lederman Managing Director FB Salons

"Johns training with my management team was excellent, it was very different from the business coaching and support I have had in the past. John was clear, thoughtful and he addressed the issues we needed to cover without us even knowing they were being addressed! His follow up has been fantastic and exactly what I needed. I would recommend John and his team to anyone looking at getting some business coaching and training done"

—Wendy Crawford, Peopleworx

"In my dealings with John as our business coach, I have found him to be a motivated and insightful agent of positive change. He is able to burrow down to the root cause of issues and introduce effective forms of measurement. John then identifies and implements practical solutions and is there to provide the gentle

persuasion required to ensure that results are achieved."
—Mark Felton, Lindale Insurances
ACCLAIM FOR JOHN MILLAR'S
Business Coaching and Training in their own words....

"You have coached and trained us so well throughout the year that we are now used to & find it easy to prepare a 90 day plan, then break it down to actionable bite size pieces. Planning in business & personal life certainly is important. It allows us to identify the important things & the bigger picture. Thank you for your support & guidance throughout the year. And not to mention your insight, external perspective to review & assist our business moving forward." — Linda Turner, Director Roy A McDonald Certified Practicing Accountants

"If you want to achieve sales results you never thought were possible and give yourself a competitive edge my strong suggestion is to engage John services and listen closely to what John has to say, during the time I was trained by John I was one of eight sales consultants in a national business for 10 out of the 13 months I lead the sales tally and in 1 quarter I generated three times the revenue of the national sales force combined. Johns training and experience was well worth the investment

and paid big dividends. Thanks John."
—Julian Fadini, Bellvue Capital

"John is a very enthusiastic trainer and business coach, he is very passionate about getting business owners and their team where they need to be. He goes the extra mile to keep ahead of the latest developments which he then uses to benefit his clients."
—Darren Reddy CPA

"I have been to a few seminars and heard John speak numerous times about sales, marketing and business. He is a very knowledgable and extremely enthusiastic business coach in all his interactions and I would recommend him to all business owners who need a sales and marketing boost!"
—Andrew Heath, Managing Director, Fresh Living Group

"I worked with John Millar and found his business knowledge, passion and innovation to be inspiring. He has always been able to set (and achieve) strategic long and short-term goals both for himself and his clients without losing that personal connection he builds with everyone he meets. He has been and I believe will continue to be a strong mentor and trainer for anyone wanting to take that next step in their business."

—Bree Webster, Online Marketing Guru

"Massive Action Day" – what an understatement, John Millars 4 hour frenzy challenged me to seriously review areas of my business I would not have gone to …. In this way, the process identified incongruence's in my mind, my business and my modus operandi. It's created a paradigm shift. Thanks John, the road map just got a whole lot clearer. Your friendship and insights since 2003 have been a gift to my business and I." —Andrew Reay, Counsellor, Hypnotherapist and Counsellor, Thinkshift Transformations

"John Millar is not your usual Business coach or trainer, he gets involved with you and your business and provides hands on help to make sure you follow through on his advice. He is highly motivated to help his clients and his personal guarantee certainly shows this. He has now transposed his thoughts, advice and love of good business onto a series of DVD's in his business venture – More Profit Less Time. This has excellent tips and advice for anyone either starting out or already in business. I highly recommend John to any business owner who wants to run a business and not a j.o.b.!"

—Darren Cassidy, Managing Director HR2U

JOHN MILLAR

www.ingramcontent.com/pod-product-compliance
Lightning Source LLC
Chambersburg PA
CBHW071832200526
45169CB00018B/1376